new bedroom design

daab

El dormitorio es el área doméstica de relajación absoluta, el lugar más privado de la casa y, por lo tanto, el más íntimo. En la actualidad, una de las tendencias con más aceptación en el diseño de dormitorios es la que elimina elementos innecesarios que dificulten la tarea del descanso y la que opta por la simplicidad de formas y los espacios diáfanos. Otro de los retos es lograr integrar el dormitorio en los nuevos tipos de viviendas surgidos con las nuevas necesidades sociales, como los lofts, los pequeños estudios, etcétera. Además, es también muy importante el uso de la luz, ya sea natural o artificial, en la creación de ambientes agradables y envolventes; por ello, algunos de los dormitorios más interesantes mostrados en el presente libro han centrado algunas de sus intervenciones arquitectónicas en este objetivo.

La chambre à coucher est la pièce de la maison consacrée au repos absolu, l'endroit le plus privé et, par conséquent le plus intime. Une des tendances actuelles les plus en vue pour le design des chambres est celle qui élimine les éléments inutiles qui rendent difficiles le repos et celle qui privilégie la simplicité des formes et les espaces diaphanes. Un autre objectif à atteindre est celui qui permet d'intégrer la chambre dans les nouveaux types d'habitat apparus avec les besoins sociaux actuels, comme les lofts, les petits studios, etc. Qu'elle soit naturelle ou artificielle, l'utilisation de la lumière est aussi très importante pour créer des ambiances agréables et captivantes; c'est pour cela que certaines chambres les plus intéressantes montrées dans ce livre ont centré quelques-unes de leurs interventions architectoniques dans ce but.

La stanza da letto é l'area domestica dell'assoluto riposo, il luogo piú privato della casa e, pertanto, il piú intimo. Attualmente una delle tendenze piú accettate nella progettazione delle stanze da letto é quella che elimina elementi innecessari che rendano difficile il riposo e che opta per la semplicitá delle forme e per gli spazi trasparenti. Un altro dei compiti della progettazione é quello di riuscire ad integrare la camera da letto nei tipi di alloggi sorti dalle nuove necessitá sociali, come i loft, i monolocali, ecc. E' inoltre di estrema importanza l'uso della luce, sia naturale che artificiale, per la creazione di ambienti gradevoli e avvolgenti; perció alcune delle stanze da letto piú interessanti presentate in questo libro hanno centrato i loro interventi architettonici su quest'obiettivo.

Das Schlafzimmer ist der Ort der absoluten Ruhe, d.h. der privateste und sicher auch der intimste Bereich jeder Wohnung. Heutzutage neigt man bei der Gestaltung von Schlafzimmern dazu, auf alle Elemente zu verzichten, die störend auf unsere Ruhe einwirken könnten. Daher wird Wert gelegt auf helle Räume mit einfacher, klarer Formgebung. Neue Formen des Wohnens, die aufgrund veränderter Lebens- und Arbeitsbedingungen entstanden sind, wie etwa Lofts oder kleine Studios, erfordern auch ein Umdenken bei der Eingliederung des Schlafzimmers. Besonders wichtig bei der Schaffung einer behaglichen Atmosphäre ist eine durchdachte Lichtführung, sei es über die Nutzung des Tageslichts oder mittels Einsatz künstlicher Lichtquellen. Bei einigen der in diesem Band vorgestellten Schlafzimmer bestimmte die Lichtführung die gesamte Gestaltungsplanung.

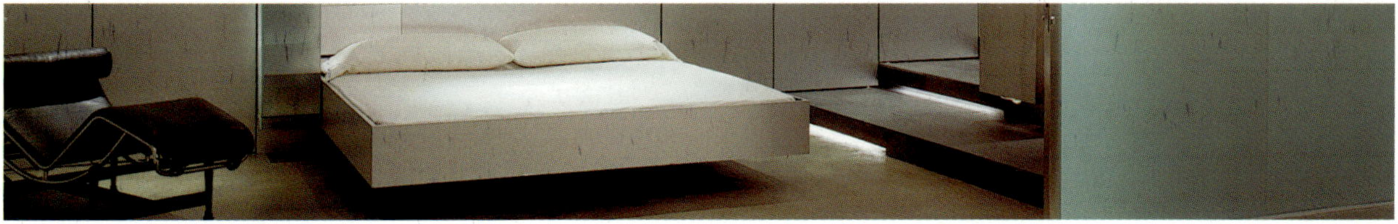

The bedroom is the domestic area designated for absolute repose, and represents the most private space inside the home, thus rendering it the most intimate. Today, one of the most common trends in bedroom design is the absence of unnecessary elements that inhibit our ability to rest and the presence of simple forms and diaphanous spaces. One of the challenges consists of integrating the bedroom into new kind of living spaces generated by evolving social patterns, such as lofts, small studios, and etcetera. The implementation of light–both natural and artificial–is also of major importance in creating pleasant and intimate spaces. For this reason, some of the most interesting bedrooms displayed in this book have focused their architectural interventions around this objective.

Attilio Stocchi | Milan, Italy

Structural Loft

Bergamo, Italy | 2002

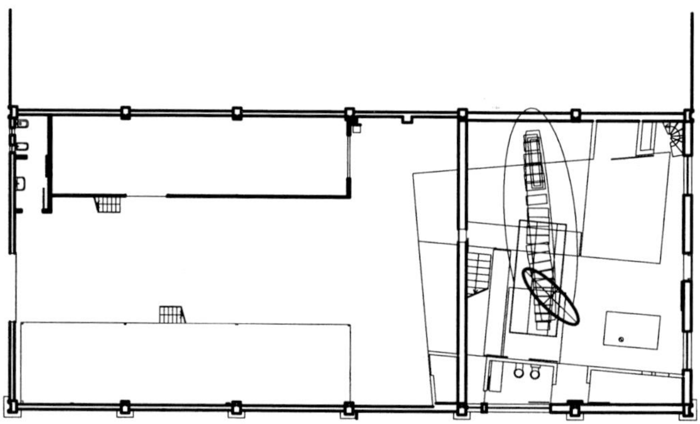

Brunete Fraccaroli | São Paulo, Brazil
House for an Executive
São Paulo, Brazil | 2003

Budji Living | Bangkok, Thailand

House in Bangkok

Bangkok, Thailand | 2001

Cigolle X Coleman Architects | Pacific Palisades, USA

TR1 House

Pacific Palisades, USA | 2001

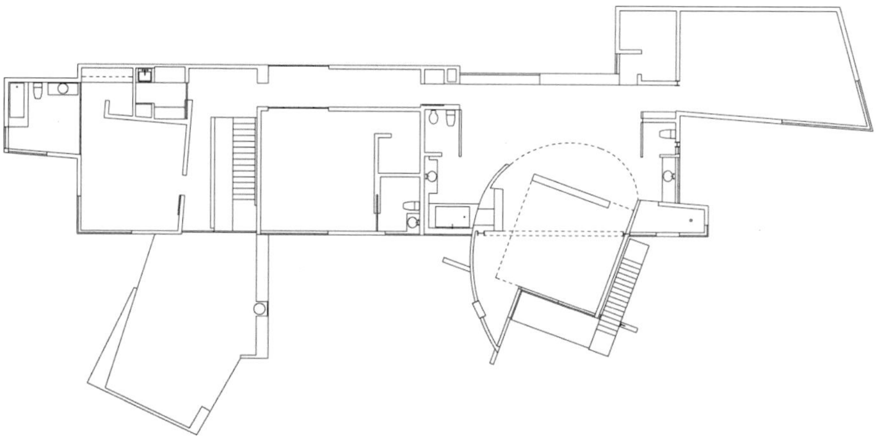

DENNIS LEHANE

Conran & Partners | London, UK
Mountain Apartment
Tokyo, Japan | 2003

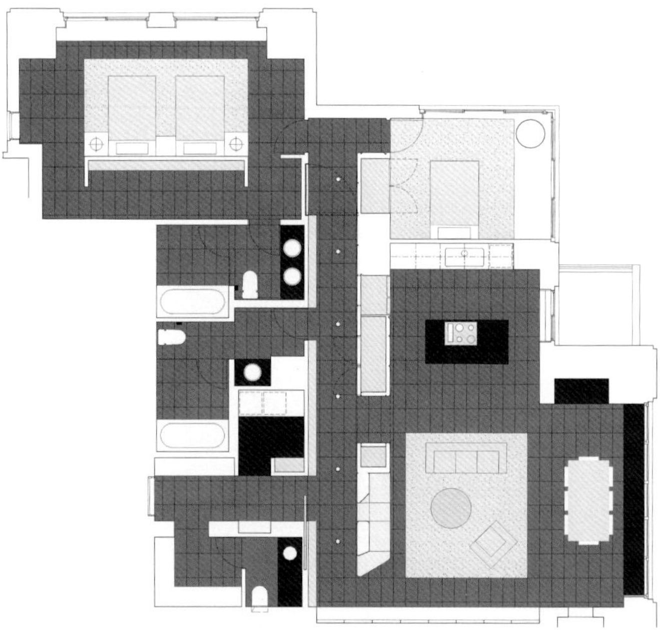

window style
RESTAURANTS

ROPPONGI
HILLS

David Ling Architect | New York, USA

Ling Loft

New York, USA | 2000

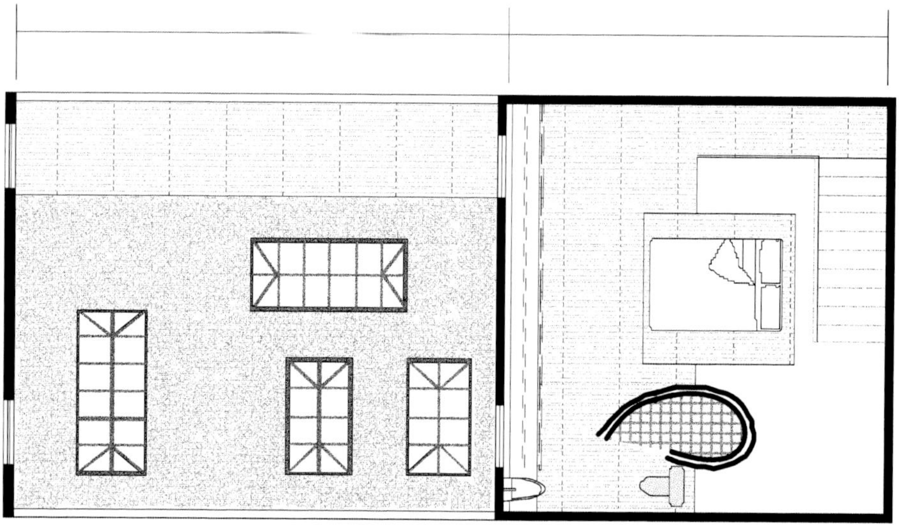

Deborah Berke | New Jersey, USA
Crosby St. Residence
New Jersey, USA | 2003

Delugan_Meissl Architects | Vienna, Austria
Ray House
Vienna, Austria | 2002

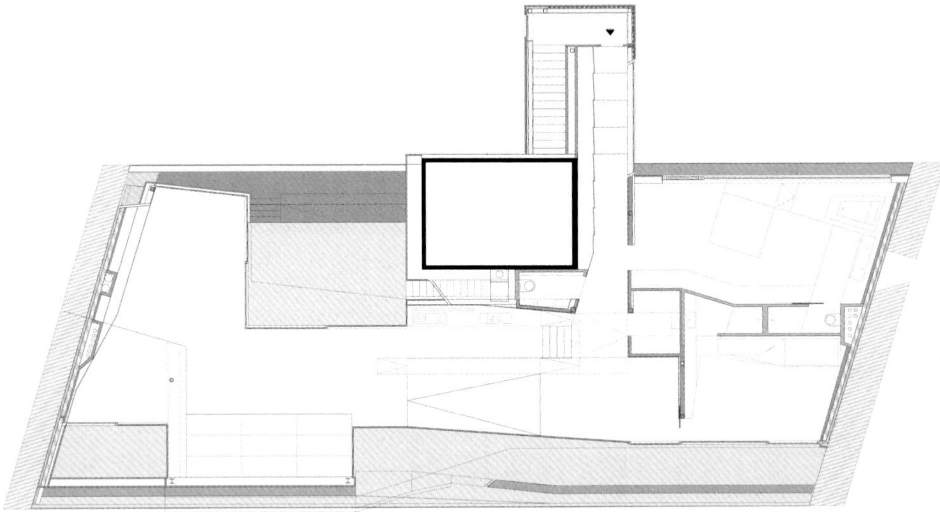

Detail | London, UK
Wapping Wall
London, UK | 2001

Deu i Deu. Estudi de Disseny | Barcelona, Spain

House in Valldoreix

Barcelona, Spain | 2003

Eric Rosen Architect | Los Angeles, USA
Ocean Avenue Residence
Los Angeles, USA | 2003

Ettore Sottsass | Milan, Italy
Olabuenaga House
Maui, Hawaii, USA | 2003

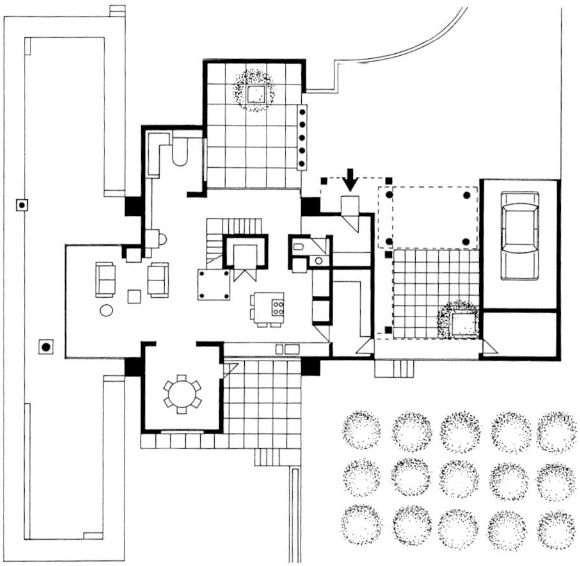

Fabrizio Leoni | Cagliari, Italy
Kbla System
Cagliari, Italy | 2003

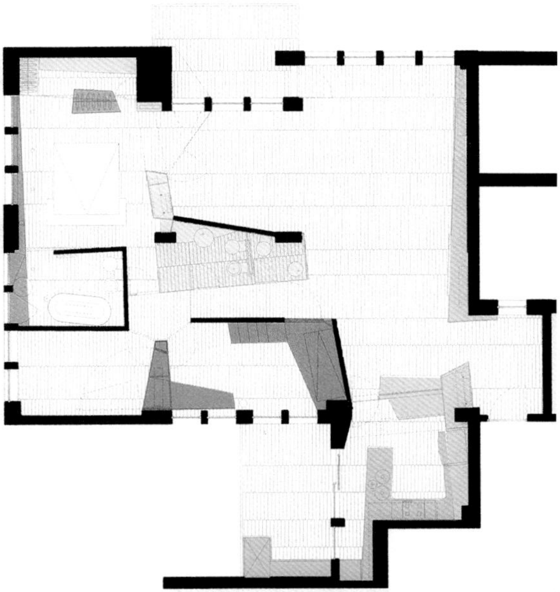

Gary Chang / EDGE (HK) LTD | Hong Kong, China
Chang Apartment
Hong Kong, China | 2002

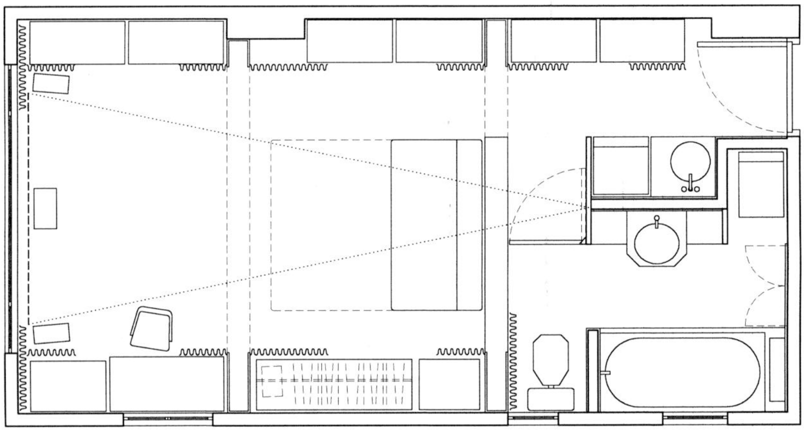

GCA Arquitectes Associats | Barcelona, Spain

Vives-Escarmis Loft

Barcelona, Spain | 2003

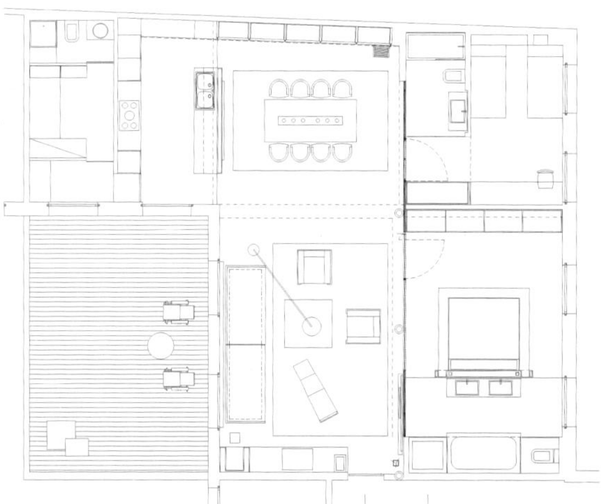

Gregory Phillips Architects | London, UK

Tabernacle Street Loft

London, UK | 2003

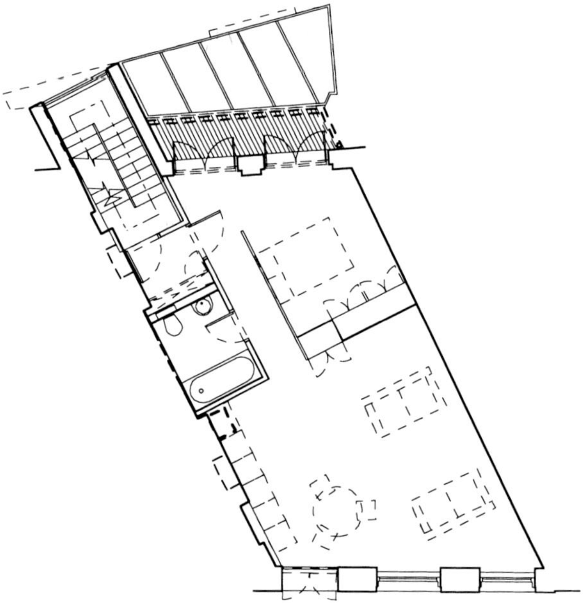

Jackson Clements Burrows | Melbourne, Australia

AKM Warehouse Apartment

Melbourne, Australia | 2004

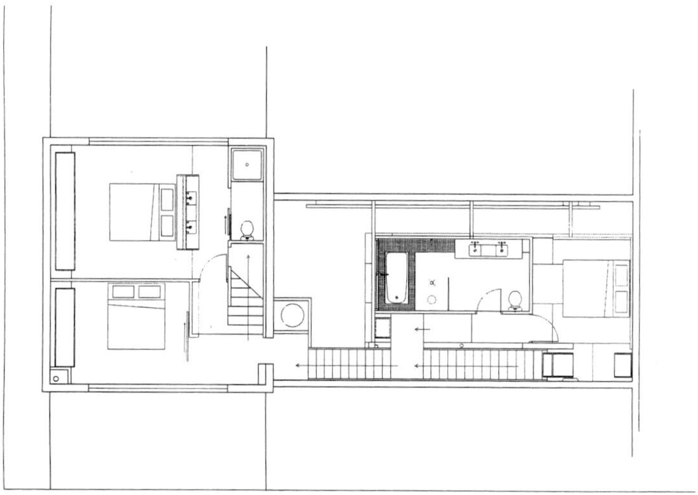

DEAVER

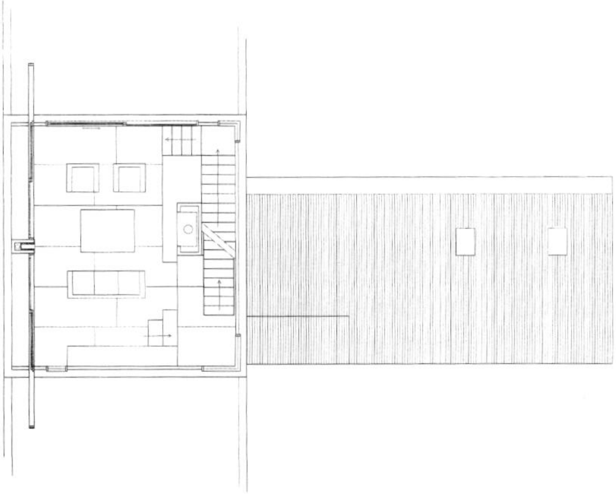

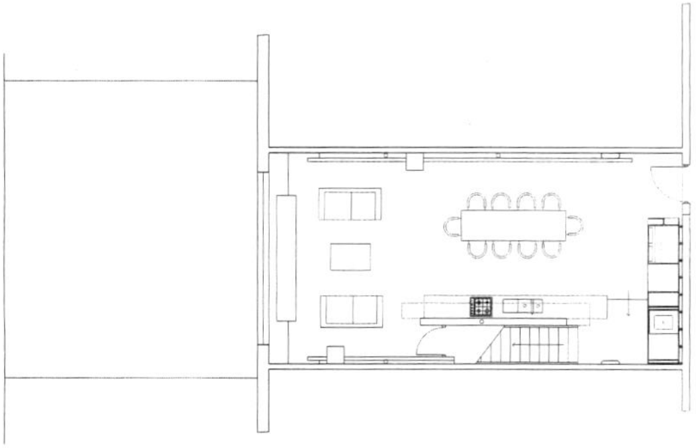

Jennifer Randall Associates | Seattle, USA

Felner Residence

Seattle, USA | 2003

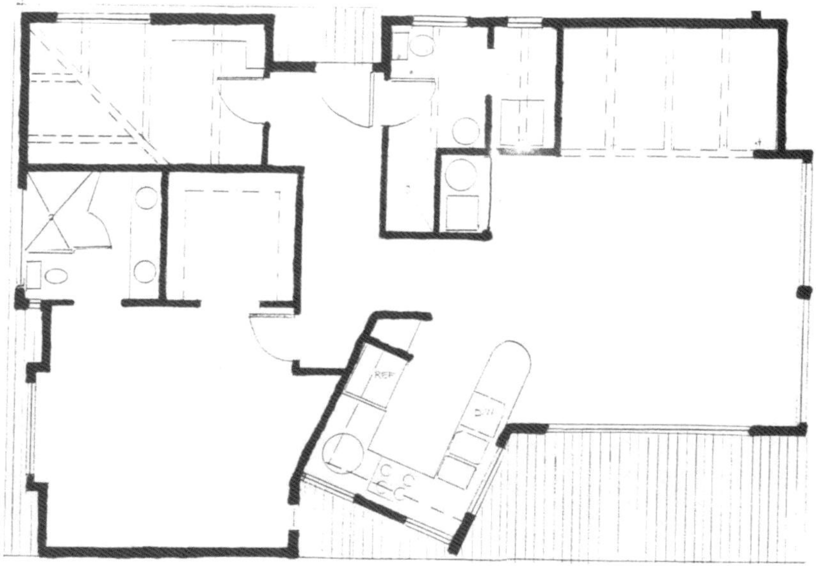

Not

the
LoSt.

Jensen & Macy Architects | San Francisco, USA

Brown Residence

San Francisco, USA | 2003

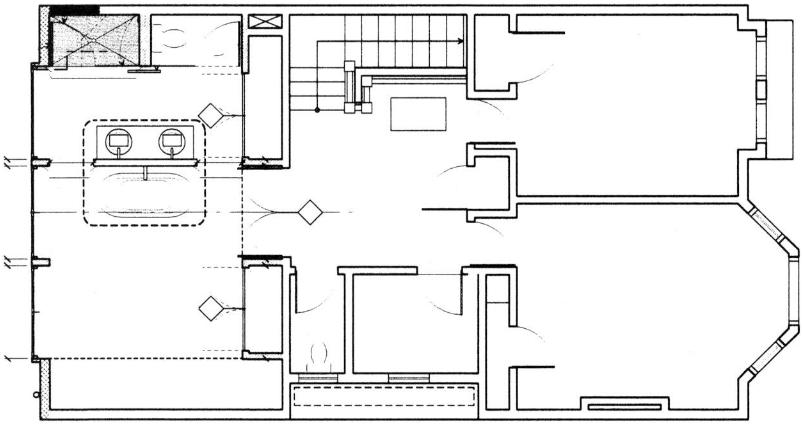

Joan Bach | Barcelona, Spain

Vallromanes House

Barcelona, Spain | 2002

Johnson Chou | Toronto, Canada
Luxurious Cell
Toronto, Canada | 2001

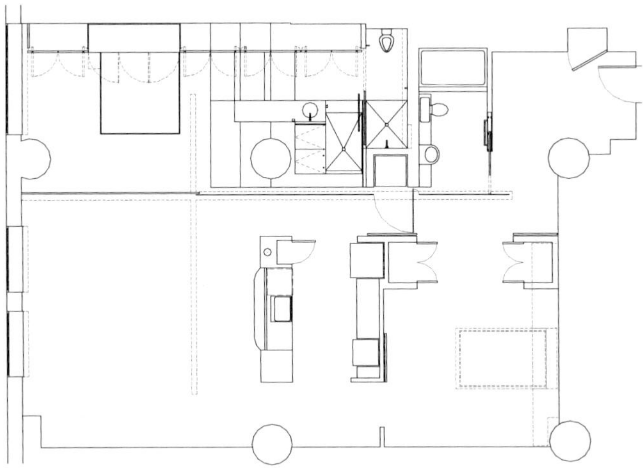

Jonathan Reed | London, UK
Flat in Berlin
Berlin, Germany | 2001

Leddy Maytum Stacy Architects | San Francisco, USA
Carmen House
Lower California, Mexico | 2001

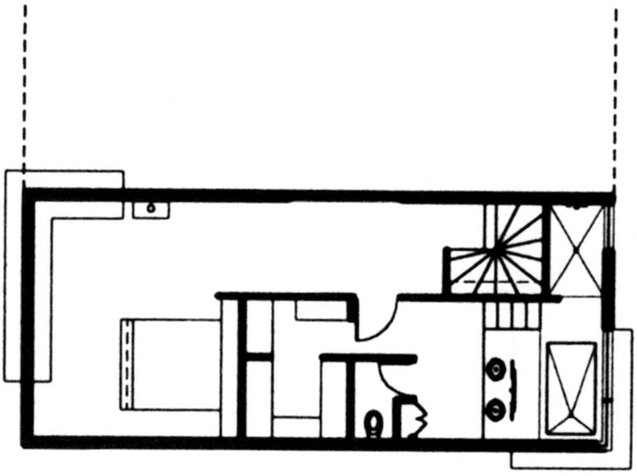

CUBA LIBRE
PATRICIA CORNWELL

Legorreta Arquitectos | Mexico D.F., Mexico
Víctor House
Valle de Bravo, Mexico | 2003

LKD Concepts | Zurich, Switzerland

House in Gordes

Gordes, France | 2001

Messana O´Rorke Architects | New York, USA

Delavan House

New York, USA | 2003

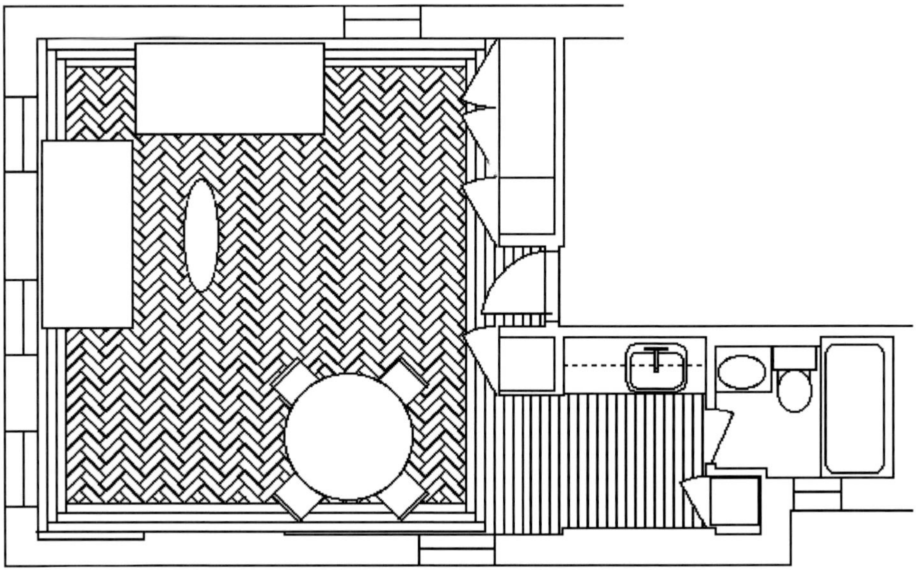

Messana O´Rorke Architects | New York, USA
Miele House
New York, USA | 2003

Michael Ryan Architect | New Jersey, USA
Martin House
New Jersey, USA | 2003

Miquel Adrià, Isaac Broid & Michel Rojkind | Mexico D.F., Mexico
F2 House
Sayavedra, Mexico | 2001

Patricia Zacek | Vienna, Austria

Renovation of a House

Vienna, Austria | 2002

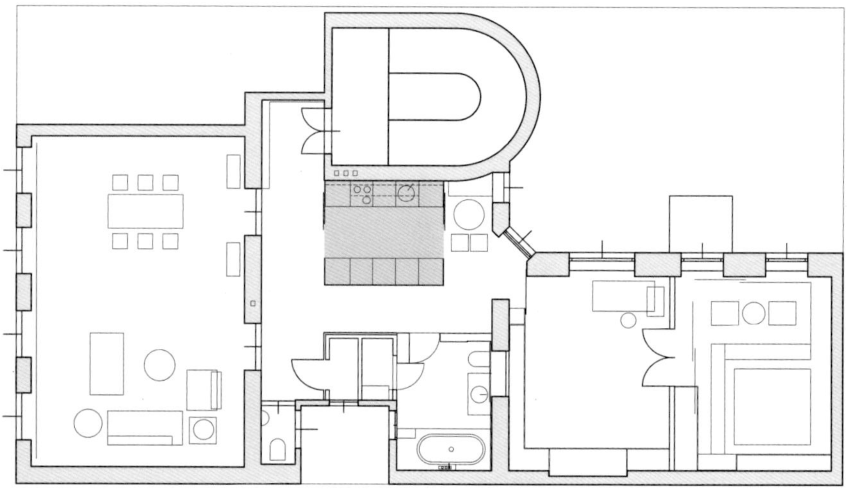

Radan Hubicka | Prague, Czec Republic
Villa Podoli
Prague, Czec Republic | 2001

Real Studios | London, UK

Le Méridien Hotel

Vienna, Austria | 2003

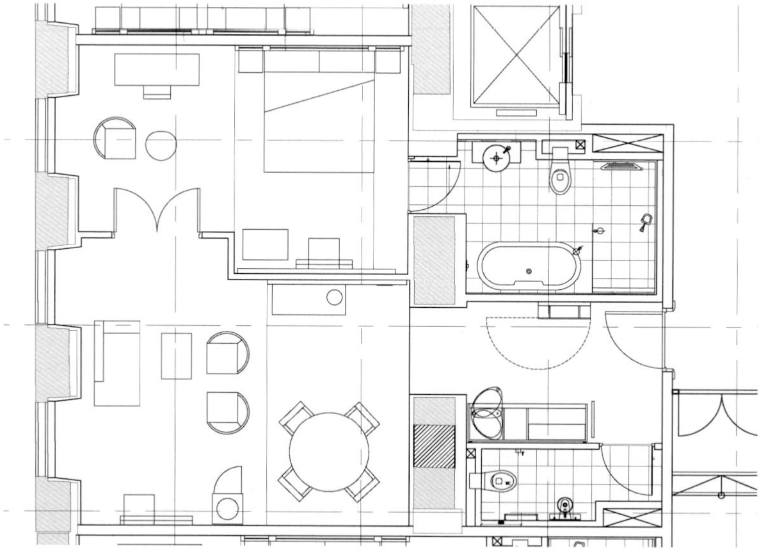

Robinson + Grisaru Architecture | New York, USA

Carlson Loft

New York, USA | 2002

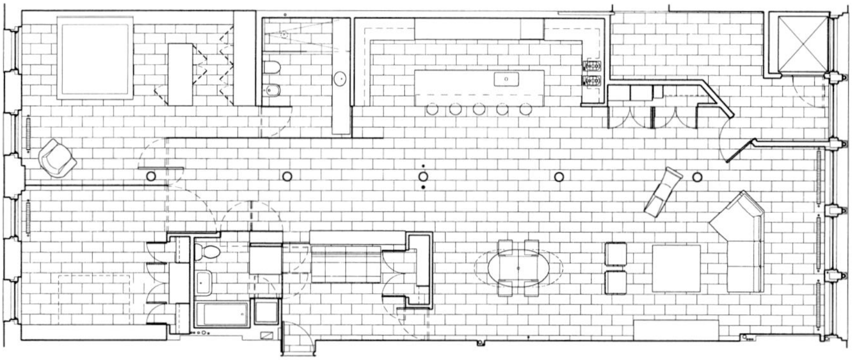

Roger Bellera | Girona, Spain
Loft in Poble Sec
Barcelona, Spain | 2003

Roger Hirsch with Myriam Corti Architect / Tocar INC Interior Design | New York, USA

Loft in Tribeca

New York, USA | 2003

Samuel Lerch | Zurich, Switzerland

Modern Zen

Zurich, Switzerland | 2003

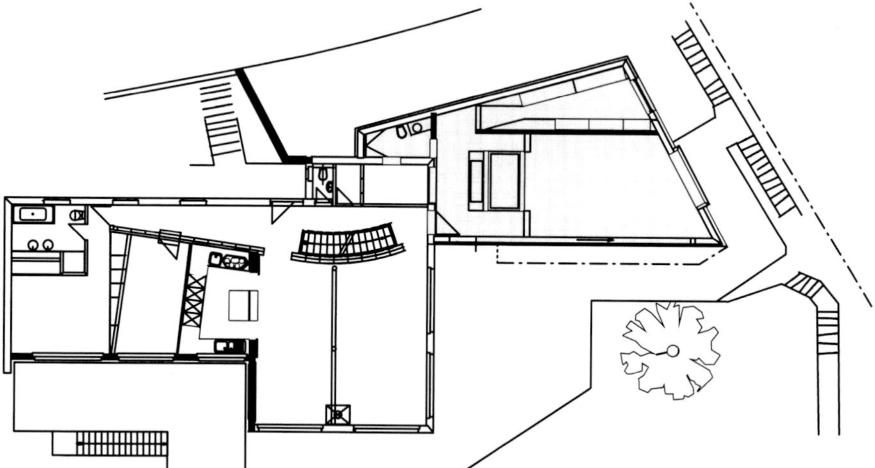

SJB Interiors | Melbourne, Australia

Melbourne Penthouse

Melbourne, Australia | 2003

BAUHAUS

Stephen Sharp | London, UK

House in Boltom Gardens

London, UK | 2003

T-HOCH-T Architektur | Vienna, Austria

Penthouse in the Lake Wörthersee

Wohnen, Austria | 2002

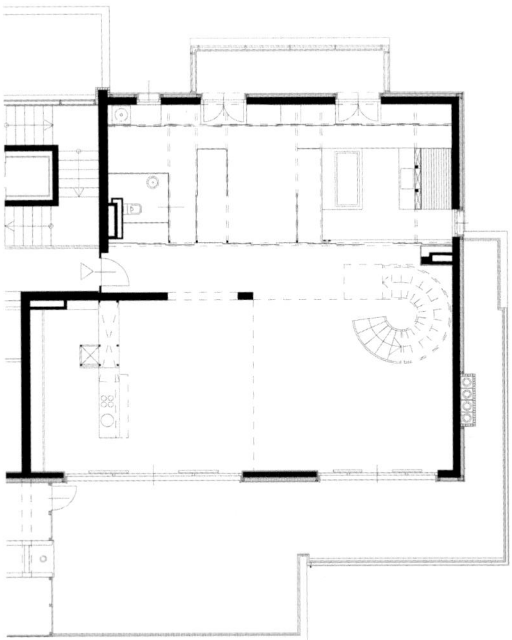

TEN Arquitectos | Colonia Condesa, Mexico
Enrique Norten House
Mexico D.F., Mexico | 2001

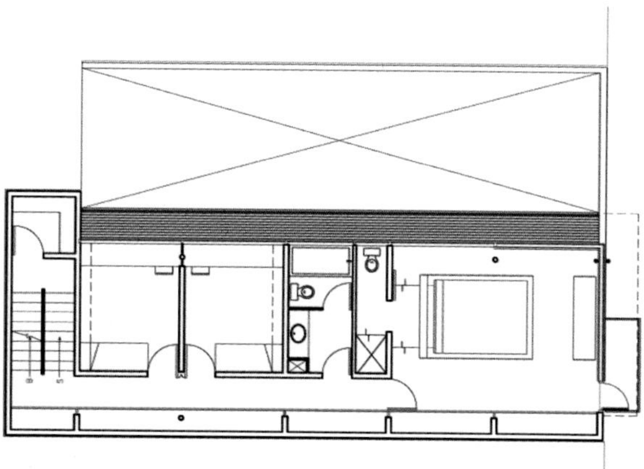

S,M,L,XL

Titan Design | Tel Aviv, Israel
White Bedroom
Tel Aviv, Israel | 2003

Tyler London | London, UK

Chelsea Apartment

London, UK | 2001

Unknown
Building Blocks
London, UK | 2001

DESIGN WEEK
Taking shape

Attilio Stocchi
Via Daverio 7, Milan 20122, Italy
P +02 551 89 184
F +02 551 89 184
Structural Loft
Photos: © Andrea Martiradonna

Brunete Fraccaroli
R. Guarará 261, 7 andar, Jd. Paulista, CEP 01425-001,
Sãu Paulo, Brazil
P +55 11 3885 8309
brunete@osite.com.br
House for an Executive
Photos: © Tuca Reinés

Budji Living
7 soi Sang-Ngern (Thonglor 25)' Sukhumvit 55 Rd.,
Klongton - Nua, Wattana, Bangkok, Thailand
P +662 712 9833
F +662 712 9834
House in Bangkok
Photos: © Zapaimages / Agi Simões

Cigolle X Coleman Architects
17463 Tramonto Drive, Pacific Palisades, CA 90272, USA
P +1 310 454 3684
www.california-architects.com / cigolle-coleman
kcoleman@usc.edu
TR1 House
Photos: © Undine Pröhl

Conran & Partners
22 Shad Thames, London SE1 2YU, UK
P +44 020 7403 88 99
www.conranandpartners.com
Mountain Apartment
Photos: © Conran & Partners

David Ling Architect
225 E 21St, New York, NY 10010, USA
P +1 212 982 7089
F +1 212 475 1336
www.inch.com
Ling Loft
Photos: © Zapaimages / Reto Guntli

Delugan_Meissl Architects
Mittersteig 13/4, A-1040 Vienna, Austria
P +43 1 585 36 90
F +43 1 585 36 90-11
www.deluganmeissl.at
Ray House
Photos: © Rupert Steiner

Deborah Berke
New Jersey, USA
Crosby St. Residence
Photos: © Catherine Tighe

Detail
D2 Metropolitan Wharf, Wapping Wall, London E1W 3SS, UK
P +44 (0) 20 74 88 16 69
F +44 (0) 20 74 88 25 24
Wapping Wall
Photos: © Jonathan Moore

Deu i Deu. Estudi de Disseny
C/ Calatrava 23, 08017 Barcelona, Spain
P +34 93 280 00 10
F +34 93 280 21 10
www.deuideu.com
House in Valldoreix
Photos: © José Luis Hausmann

Eric Rosen Architect
11525 Washington Blvd., Los Angeles, CA 90066, USA
P +1 310 313 3052
F +1 310 313 3062
www.ericrosen.com
Ocean Avenue Residence
Photos: © Erich Koyama

Ettore Sottsass / Sottsass Associati E.E.I.G.
Via Melone 2, 20121 Milan, Italy
P +39 02 809596
F +39 02 809596
www.sotsass.it
Olabuenaga House
Photos: © Undine Pröhl

Fabrizio Leoni Architetto
Via Riva Villasanta 45, 09134 Cagliari, Italy
P +39 348 22 54 073 / +34 600 059 586
fabricio_leoni@hotmail.com
Kbla System
Photos: © Dessi e Monari

Gary Chang / EDGE (HK) Ltd
Hong Kong, China
Chang Apartment
Photos: © Almond Chu

GCA Arquitectes Associats
C/ Valencia 289, bajos, 08009 Barcelona, Spain
P +34 93 476 18 00
F +34 93 476 18 06
www.gcaarq.com
lec@gcaarq.com
Vives-Escarmis Loft
Photos: © Jordi Miralles

Gregory Phillips Architecs
66 Great Cumberland Place, London W1H 7FD, UK
P +44 207 724 3040
www.gregoryphillips.com
Tabernacle Street Loft
Photos: © Paul Smoothy

Jackson Clements Burrows
One Harwood Place, Melbourne 300, Australia
P +03 96 54 6227
F +03 96 54 6195
www.jcba.com.au
AKM Warehouse Apartment
Photos: © Trevor Mein

Jennifer Randall Associates
1100 East Union, 1B, Seattle WA 98122, USA
P +1 206 323 1520
F +1 206 325 2306
www.jradesigns.com
Felner Residence
Photos: © Jordi Miralles

Jensen & Macy Architects
55 Sumner Street, San Francisco, CA 94103, USA
P +1 415 553 36 50
Brown Residence
Photos: © Jensen & Macy Architects

Joan Bach
Barcelona, Spain
P +34 93 488 19 25
Vallromanes House
Photos: © Jordi Miralles

Johnson Chou
Toronto, Canada
Luxurious Cell
Photos: © Volker Seding Photography

Jonathan Reed
151 a Sydney Street, London SW3, UK
P +44 20 75 65 00 66
studio@studioreed.com
Flat in Berlin
Photos: © Red Cover / Ken Hayden

Leddy Maytum Stacy Architects
677 Harrison Street, San Francisco, CA 94107, USA
P +1 415 495 1700
www.lmsarch.com
Carmen House
Photos: © Undine Pröhl

Legorreta Arquitectos
Palacio de Versalles 285 'A', Mexico D.F. 11020, Mexico
P +52 55 251-96-98
legorret@lmasl.com.mx
Víctor House
Photos: © Adam Butler

LKD Concepts
Neuhausstrasse, 3, 6318 Zug, Switzerland
P/F +41 41 758 22 49
House in Gordes
Photos: © Zapaimages / Reto Guntli

Messana O´Rorke Architects
118 West 22nd Street, 9 floor, New York, NY 10011, USA
P +1 212 807 19 60
www.messanaororke.com
Delavan House
Miele House
Photos: © Elizabeth Felicella

Michael Ryan Architect
New Jersey, USA
Martin House
Photos: © Catherine Tighe

Miquel Adrià, Isaac Broid & Michel Rojkind
Campos Eliseos 432, Polanco, Mexico D.F. 11560, Mexico
P + 5280 85 21
F + 5280 80 21
F2 House
Photos: © Undine Pröhl

Patricia Zacek
Gobergasse 65 / 2, A-1130 Vienna, Austria
P +01 879 80 20
F +01 876 00 50
www.patricia-zacek.at
Renovation of a House
Photos: © Rupert Steiner

Radan Hubicka
Wenzigova 17, 120 00, Prague 2, Czech Republic
P +420 224 261 076
F +420 224 261 077
www.arch.cz/aarh
radan.hubicka@iol.cz
Villa Podoli
Photos: © Artur / Robertino Nikolic

Real Studios
64 Great Suffolk Street, London SE1 OBL, UK
P +44 20 79 28 22 11
F +44 20 79 28 77 11
www.realstudios.co.uk
Le Méridien Hotel
Photos: © Zapaimages / Reto Guntli

Robinson + Grisaru Architecture
70 Washington Street, Suite 1013, New York, NY 11201, USA
r.grisaru@rgarch.com
Carlson Loft
Photos: © Michael Moran

Roger Bellera
Plaça de l'Església, s/n., Galeries Begur, Local 3,
17255 Begur, Girona, Spain
P +34 629 78 31 12
Loft in Poble Sec
Photos: © Jordi Miralles

Roger Hirsch with Myriam Corti
91 Crosby Street, New York, NY 10012, USA
P +1 212 219 2609
F +1 212 219 2767
www.rogerhirsch.com / www.tocardesign.com
Loft in Tribeca
Photos: © Michael Moran

Samuel Lerch
Zurich, Switzerland
P +41 (0) 1 382 46 55
Modern Zen
Photos: © Zapaimages / Bruno Helbling

SJB Interiors
25 Coventry Street, Southbank, VIC 3006, Australia
P +61 3 9686 2122
www.sjb.com.au
Melbourne Penthouse
Photos: © Tony Miller

Stephen Sharp
London, UK
steven.bramham@ntlworld.com
House in Boltom Gardens
Photos: © Red Cover / Jake Fitzjones

T-HOCH-T Architektur
Heumühlgasse 10, 1040 Vienna, Austria
P +01 798 79 80
F +01 798 79 80-40
www.t-hoch-n.com
Penthouse in the Lake Wörthersee
Photos: © Rupert Steiner

TEN Arquitectos
Cuernavaca 114-PB, Colonia Condesa,
Mexico D.F. 06140, Mexico
P + 52 55 5211 8004
F + 52 55 5286 1735
www.ten-arquitectos.com
Enrique Norten House
Photos: © Undine Pröhl

Titan Design
Yedidia Frenkel (Emek Israel) 14, Tel Aviv, Israel
P +972 3 518 7101
F +972 3 518 7514
White Bedroom
Photos: © Yael Pincus

Tyler London
22a Ives Street, London SW3 2ND, UK
P +44 20 75 81 36 77
F +44 20 75 81 81 15
www.tylerlondon.com
Chelsea Apartment
Photos: © Adam Butler

Unknown
London, UK
Building Blocks
Photos: © Red Cover / Nick Carter

published and distributed worldwide by
daab gmbh
stadtwaldgürtel 57
d - 50935 köln

p +49-221-94 10 740
f +49-221-94 10 741

mail@daab-online.de
www.daab-online.de

publisher ralf daab
rdaab@daab-online.de

art director feyyaz
mail@feyyaz.com

editorial project by loft publications

editor Encarna Castillo
layout Diego González
english translation Ana Cristina G. Cañizares
french translation Jean Pierre Layre Cassou
italian translation Grazia Suffritti
german translation Martin Fischer
copy editing Raquel Vicente Durán

printed in spain
Anman Gràfiques del Vallès, Spain
www.anman.com

isbn 3-937718-16-8
d.l.: B-27636-04